Books I've Read

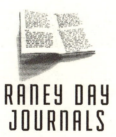

RANEY DAY JOURNALS

Copyright © 2021 Ken & Deborah Raney

All rights reserved.
No part of this book may be reproduced
or used in any manner without
written permission of the copyright owner.

DATE STARTED	TITLE:
	AUTHOR:
DATE FINISHED	GENRE:
	NOTES / REVIEW:
RATING ★★★★★	

DATE STARTED	TITLE:
	AUTHOR:
DATE FINISHED	GENRE:
	NOTES / REVIEW:
RATING ★★★★★	

DATE STARTED	TITLE:
	AUTHOR:
DATE FINISHED	GENRE:
	NOTES / REVIEW:
RATING ★★★★★	

DATE STARTED

_____

DATE FINISHED

_____

RATING
★ ★ ★ ★ ★

TITLE: _____
AUTHOR: _____
GENRE: _____
NOTES / REVIEW: _____
_____
_____
_____

DATE STARTED

_____

DATE FINISHED

_____

RATING
★ ★ ★ ★ ★

TITLE: _____
AUTHOR: _____
GENRE: _____
NOTES / REVIEW: _____
_____
_____
_____

DATE STARTED

_____

DATE FINISHED

_____

RATING
★ ★ ★ ★ ★

TITLE: _____
AUTHOR: _____
GENRE: _____
NOTES / REVIEW: _____
_____
_____
_____

DATE STARTED	TITLE:
	AUTHOR:
DATE FINISHED	GENRE:
	NOTES / REVIEW:
RATING	

DATE STARTED	TITLE:
	AUTHOR:
DATE FINISHED	GENRE:
	NOTES / REVIEW:
RATING	

DATE STARTED	TITLE:
	AUTHOR:
DATE FINISHED	GENRE:
	NOTES / REVIEW:
RATING	

Date started

_____

Date finished

_____

rating

★ ★ ★ ★ ★

TITLE:

AUTHOR:

GENRE:

NOTES / REVIEW:

Date started

_____

Date finished

_____

rating

★ ★ ★ ★ ★

TITLE:

AUTHOR:

GENRE:

NOTES / REVIEW:

Date started

_____

Date finished

_____

rating

★ ★ ★ ★ ★

TITLE:

AUTHOR:

GENRE:

NOTES / REVIEW:

DATE STARTED _____ **DATE FINISHED** _____ RATING ★ ★ ★ ★ ★	TITLE: AUTHOR: GENRE: NOTES / REVIEW:
DATE STARTED _____ **DATE FINISHED** _____ RATING ★ ★ ★ ★ ★	TITLE: AUTHOR: GENRE: NOTES / REVIEW:
DATE STARTED _____ **DATE FINISHED** _____ RATING ★ ★ ★ ★ ★	TITLE: AUTHOR: GENRE: NOTES / REVIEW:

Date started	Title:
	Author:
Date finished	Genre:
	Notes / Review:
Rating	
★★★★★	

Date started	Title:
	Author:
Date finished	Genre:
	Notes / Review:
Rating	
★★★★★	

Date started	Title:
	Author:
Date finished	Genre:
	Notes / Review:
Rating	
★★★★★	

DATE STARTED	TITLE:
————————	AUTHOR:
DATE FINISHED	GENRE:
————————	NOTES / REVIEW:
RATING ★★★★★	

DATE STARTED	TITLE:
————————	AUTHOR:
DATE FINISHED	GENRE:
————————	NOTES / REVIEW:
RATING ★★★★★	

DATE STARTED	TITLE:
————————	AUTHOR:
DATE FINISHED	GENRE:
————————	NOTES / REVIEW:
RATING ★★★★★	

Date started

_____

Date finished

_____

Rating
☆☆☆☆☆

Title: _____
Author: _____
Genre: _____
Notes / Review: _____
_____
_____
_____

Date started

_____

Date finished

_____

Rating
☆☆☆☆☆

Title: _____
Author: _____
Genre: _____
Notes / Review: _____
_____
_____
_____

Date started

_____

Date finished

_____

Rating
☆☆☆☆☆

Title: _____
Author: _____
Genre: _____
Notes / Review: _____
_____
_____
_____

DATE STARTED

DATE FINISHED

RATING

TITLE:

AUTHOR:

GENRE:

NOTES / REVIEW:

DATE STARTED

DATE FINISHED

RATING

TITLE:

AUTHOR:

GENRE:

NOTES / REVIEW:

DATE STARTED

DATE FINISHED

RATING

TITLE:

AUTHOR:

GENRE:

NOTES / REVIEW:

DATE STARTED

DATE FINISHED

RATING
★★★★★

TITLE:
AUTHOR:
GENRE:
NOTES / REVIEW:

DATE STARTED

DATE FINISHED

RATING
★★★★★

TITLE:
AUTHOR:
GENRE:
NOTES / REVIEW:

DATE STARTED

DATE FINISHED

RATING
★★★★★

TITLE:
AUTHOR:
GENRE:
NOTES / REVIEW:

Date started

_____

Date finished

_____

Rating

★ ★ ★ ★ ★

Title: _____
Author: _____
Genre: _____
Notes / Review: _____
_____
_____
_____

Date started

_____

Date finished

_____

Rating

★ ★ ★ ★ ★

Title: _____
Author: _____
Genre: _____
Notes / Review: _____
_____
_____
_____

Date started

_____

Date finished

_____

Rating

★ ★ ★ ★ ★

Title: _____
Author: _____
Genre: _____
Notes / Review: _____
_____
_____
_____

DATE STARTED
_____

DATE FINISHED
_____

RATING
★★★★★

TITLE: _____
AUTHOR: _____
GENRE: _____
NOTES / REVIEW: _____
_____
_____
_____

DATE STARTED
_____

DATE FINISHED
_____

RATING
★★★★★

TITLE: _____
AUTHOR: _____
GENRE: _____
NOTES / REVIEW: _____
_____
_____
_____

DATE STARTED
_____

DATE FINISHED
_____

RATING
★★★★★

TITLE: _____
AUTHOR: _____
GENRE: _____
NOTES / REVIEW: _____
_____
_____
_____

DATE STARTED

_____

DATE FINISHED

_____

RATING

★ ★ ★ ★ ★

TITLE:
AUTHOR:
GENRE:
NOTES / REVIEW:

DATE STARTED

_____

DATE FINISHED

_____

RATING

★ ★ ★ ★ ★

TITLE:
AUTHOR:
GENRE:
NOTES / REVIEW:

DATE STARTED

_____

DATE FINISHED

_____

RATING

★ ★ ★ ★ ★

TITLE:
AUTHOR:
GENRE:
NOTES / REVIEW:

DATE STARTED	TITLE:
	AUTHOR:
DATE FINISHED	GENRE:
	NOTES / REVIEW:
RATING ★★★★★	

DATE STARTED	TITLE:
	AUTHOR:
DATE FINISHED	GENRE:
	NOTES / REVIEW:
RATING ★★★★★	

DATE STARTED	TITLE:
	AUTHOR:
DATE FINISHED	GENRE:
	NOTES / REVIEW:
RATING ★★★★★	

DATE STARTED	TITLE:
	AUTHOR:
DATE FINISHED	GENRE:
	NOTES / REVIEW:
RATING ★★★★★	

DATE STARTED	TITLE:
	AUTHOR:
DATE FINISHED	GENRE:
	NOTES / REVIEW:
RATING ★★★★★	

DATE STARTED	TITLE:
	AUTHOR:
DATE FINISHED	GENRE:
	NOTES / REVIEW:
RATING ★★★★★	

Date started

Date finished

Rating
★★★★★

TITLE:
AUTHOR:
GENRE:
NOTES / REVIEW:

Date started

Date finished

Rating
★★★★★

TITLE:
AUTHOR:
GENRE:
NOTES / REVIEW:

Date started

Date finished

Rating
★★★★★

TITLE:
AUTHOR:
GENRE:
NOTES / REVIEW:

DATE STARTED	TITLE:
	AUTHOR:
DATE FINISHED	GENRE:
	NOTES / REVIEW:
RATING ★★★★★	

DATE STARTED	TITLE:
	AUTHOR:
DATE FINISHED	GENRE:
	NOTES / REVIEW:
RATING ★★★★★	

DATE STARTED	TITLE:
	AUTHOR:
DATE FINISHED	GENRE:
	NOTES / REVIEW:
RATING ★★★★★	

Date started

_____

date finished

_____

rating

★ ★ ★ ★ ★

TITLE: _____

AUTHOR: _____

GENRE: _____

NOTES / REVIEW: _____

_____

_____

_____

Date started

_____

date finished

_____

rating

★ ★ ★ ★ ★

TITLE: _____

AUTHOR: _____

GENRE: _____

NOTES / REVIEW: _____

_____

_____

_____

Date started

_____

date finished

_____

rating

★ ★ ★ ★ ★

TITLE: _____

AUTHOR: _____

GENRE: _____

NOTES / REVIEW: _____

_____

_____

_____

DATE STARTED

DATE FINISHED

RATING
★★★★★

TITLE:
AUTHOR:
GENRE:
NOTES / REVIEW:

DATE STARTED

DATE FINISHED

RATING
★★★★★

TITLE:
AUTHOR:
GENRE:
NOTES / REVIEW:

DATE STARTED

DATE FINISHED

RATING
★★★★★

TITLE:
AUTHOR:
GENRE:
NOTES / REVIEW:

Date started

_____

Date finished

_____

Rating
☆ ☆ ☆ ☆ ☆

Title: _____
Author: _____
Genre: _____
Notes / Review: _____
_____
_____

Date started

_____

Date finished

_____

Rating
☆ ☆ ☆ ☆ ☆

Title: _____
Author: _____
Genre: _____
Notes / Review: _____
_____
_____

Date started

_____

Date finished

_____

Rating
☆ ☆ ☆ ☆ ☆

Title: _____
Author: _____
Genre: _____
Notes / Review: _____
_____
_____

DATE STARTED	TITLE:
	AUTHOR:
DATE FINISHED	GENRE:
	NOTES / REVIEW:
RATING	
★★★★★	

DATE STARTED	TITLE:
	AUTHOR:
DATE FINISHED	GENRE:
	NOTES / REVIEW:
RATING	
★★★★★	

DATE STARTED	TITLE:
	AUTHOR:
DATE FINISHED	GENRE:
	NOTES / REVIEW:
RATING	
★★★★★	

DATE STARTED	TITLE:
	AUTHOR:
DATE FINISHED	GENRE:
	NOTES / REVIEW:
RATING	
★★★★★	

DATE STARTED	TITLE:
	AUTHOR:
DATE FINISHED	GENRE:
	NOTES / REVIEW:
RATING	
★★★★★	

DATE STARTED	TITLE:
	AUTHOR:
DATE FINISHED	GENRE:
	NOTES / REVIEW:
RATING	
★★★★★	

Date started

---

date finished

RATING
★★★★★

TITLE:
AUTHOR:
GENRE:
NOTES / REVIEW:

Date started

---

date finished

RATING
★★★★★

TITLE:
AUTHOR:
GENRE:
NOTES / REVIEW:

Date started

---

date finished

RATING
★★★★★

TITLE:
AUTHOR:
GENRE:
NOTES / REVIEW:

DATE STARTED	TITLE:
	AUTHOR:
DATE FINISHED	GENRE:
	NOTES / REVIEW:
RATING	
★★★★★	

DATE STARTED	TITLE:
	AUTHOR:
DATE FINISHED	GENRE:
	NOTES / REVIEW:
RATING	
★★★★★	

DATE STARTED	TITLE:
	AUTHOR:
DATE FINISHED	GENRE:
	NOTES / REVIEW:
RATING	
★★★★★	

DATE STARTED	TITLE:
DATE FINISHED	AUTHOR:
	GENRE:
RATING	NOTES / REVIEW:

DATE STARTED	TITLE:
DATE FINISHED	AUTHOR:
	GENRE:
RATING	NOTES / REVIEW:

DATE STARTED	TITLE:
DATE FINISHED	AUTHOR:
	GENRE:
RATING	NOTES / REVIEW:

Date started

date finished

rating

TITLE:
AUTHOR:
GENRE:
NOTES / REVIEW:

Date started

date finished

rating

TITLE:
AUTHOR:
GENRE:
NOTES / REVIEW:

Date started

date finished

rating

TITLE:
AUTHOR:
GENRE:
NOTES / REVIEW:

Date started

———————

Date finished

———————

rating
★★★★★

TITLE: _____
AUTHOR: _____
GENRE: _____
NOTES / REVIEW: _____
_____
_____

Date started

———————

Date finished

———————

rating
★★★★★

TITLE: _____
AUTHOR: _____
GENRE: _____
NOTES / REVIEW: _____
_____
_____

Date started

———————

Date finished

———————

rating
★★★★★

TITLE: _____
AUTHOR: _____
GENRE: _____
NOTES / REVIEW: _____
_____
_____

Date started

_____

date finished

_____

rating
★ ★ ★ ★ ★

TITLE:
AUTHOR:
GENRE:
NOTES / REVIEW:

Date started

_____

date finished

_____

rating
★ ★ ★ ★ ★

TITLE:
AUTHOR:
GENRE:
NOTES / REVIEW:

Date started

_____

date finished

_____

rating
★ ★ ★ ★ ★

TITLE:
AUTHOR:
GENRE:
NOTES / REVIEW:

Date started

_____

date finished

_____

rating
☆☆☆☆☆

TITLE:

AUTHOR:

GENRE:

NOTES / REVIEW:

Date started

_____

date finished

_____

rating
☆☆☆☆☆

TITLE:

AUTHOR:

GENRE:

NOTES / REVIEW:

Date started

_____

date finished

_____

rating
☆☆☆☆☆

TITLE:

AUTHOR:

GENRE:

NOTES / REVIEW:

Date started

Date finished

Rating

★★★★★

TITLE:
AUTHOR:
GENRE:
NOTES / REVIEW:

Date started

Date finished

Rating

★★★★★

TITLE:
AUTHOR:
GENRE:
NOTES / REVIEW:

Date started

Date finished

Rating

★★★★★

TITLE:
AUTHOR:
GENRE:
NOTES / REVIEW:

Date started	Title:
	Author:
Date finished	Genre:
	Notes / Review:
Rating	
☆☆☆☆☆	

Date started	Title:
	Author:
Date finished	Genre:
	Notes / Review:
Rating	
☆☆☆☆☆	

Date started	Title:
	Author:
Date finished	Genre:
	Notes / Review:
Rating	
☆☆☆☆☆	

DATE STARTED
_____

DATE FINISHED
_____

RATING
★ ★ ★ ★ ★

TITLE: _____
AUTHOR: _____
GENRE: _____
NOTES / REVIEW: _____
_____
_____
_____

DATE STARTED
_____

DATE FINISHED
_____

RATING
★ ★ ★ ★ ★

TITLE: _____
AUTHOR: _____
GENRE: _____
NOTES / REVIEW: _____
_____
_____
_____

DATE STARTED
_____

DATE FINISHED
_____

RATING
★ ★ ★ ★ ★

TITLE: _____
AUTHOR: _____
GENRE: _____
NOTES / REVIEW: _____
_____
_____
_____

DATE STARTED

DATE FINISHED

RATING

TITLE:
AUTHOR:
GENRE:
NOTES / REVIEW:

DATE STARTED

DATE FINISHED

RATING

TITLE:
AUTHOR:
GENRE:
NOTES / REVIEW:

DATE STARTED

DATE FINISHED

RATING

TITLE:
AUTHOR:
GENRE:
NOTES / REVIEW:

Date started

_____

Date finished

_____

Rating
★ ★ ★ ★ ★

Title: _____
Author: _____
Genre: _____
Notes / Review: _____
_____
_____
_____

Date started

_____

Date finished

_____

Rating
★ ★ ★ ★ ★

Title: _____
Author: _____
Genre: _____
Notes / Review: _____
_____
_____
_____

Date started

_____

Date finished

_____

Rating
★ ★ ★ ★ ★

Title: _____
Author: _____
Genre: _____
Notes / Review: _____
_____
_____
_____

DATE STARTED	TITLE:
DATE FINISHED	AUTHOR:
	GENRE:
RATING	NOTES / REVIEW:
★★★★★	

DATE STARTED	TITLE:
DATE FINISHED	AUTHOR:
	GENRE:
RATING	NOTES / REVIEW:
★★★★★	

DATE STARTED	TITLE:
DATE FINISHED	AUTHOR:
	GENRE:
RATING	NOTES / REVIEW:
★★★★★	

DATE STARTED	TITLE:
	AUTHOR:
DATE FINISHED	GENRE:
	NOTES / REVIEW:
RATING	
★★★★★	

DATE STARTED	TITLE:
	AUTHOR:
DATE FINISHED	GENRE:
	NOTES / REVIEW:
RATING	
★★★★★	

DATE STARTED	TITLE:
	AUTHOR:
DATE FINISHED	GENRE:
	NOTES / REVIEW:
RATING	
★★★★★	

Date started

_____

Date finished

_____

rating

TITLE:
AUTHOR:
GENRE:
NOTES / REVIEW:

Date started

_____

Date finished

_____

rating

TITLE:
AUTHOR:
GENRE:
NOTES / REVIEW:

Date started

_____

Date finished

_____

rating

TITLE:
AUTHOR:
GENRE:
NOTES / REVIEW:

DATE STARTED	TITLE:
	AUTHOR:
DATE FINISHED	GENRE:
	NOTES / REVIEW:
RATING ★★★★★	

DATE STARTED	TITLE:
	AUTHOR:
DATE FINISHED	GENRE:
	NOTES / REVIEW:
RATING ★★★★★	

DATE STARTED	TITLE:
	AUTHOR:
DATE FINISHED	GENRE:
	NOTES / REVIEW:
RATING ★★★★★	

Date started

date finished

RATING

TITLE:

AUTHOR:

GENRE:

NOTES / REVIEW:

Date started

date finished

RATING

TITLE:

AUTHOR:

GENRE:

NOTES / REVIEW:

Date started

date finished

RATING

TITLE:

AUTHOR:

GENRE:

NOTES / REVIEW:

Date started
_____

Date finished
_____

Rating
★ ★ ★ ★ ★

Title: _____
Author: _____
Genre: _____
Notes / Review: _____
_____
_____

Date started
_____

Date finished
_____

Rating
★ ★ ★ ★ ★

Title: _____
Author: _____
Genre: _____
Notes / Review: _____
_____
_____

Date started
_____

Date finished
_____

Rating
★ ★ ★ ★ ★

Title: _____
Author: _____
Genre: _____
Notes / Review: _____
_____
_____

Date Started	TITLE:
_____	AUTHOR:
Date Finished	GENRE:
_____	NOTES / REVIEW:
RATING ★★★★★	

Date Started	TITLE:
_____	AUTHOR:
Date Finished	GENRE:
_____	NOTES / REVIEW:
RATING ★★★★★	

Date Started	TITLE:
_____	AUTHOR:
Date Finished	GENRE:
_____	NOTES / REVIEW:
RATING ★★★★★	

DATE STARTED

DATE FINISHED

RATING

TITLE:

AUTHOR:

GENRE:

NOTES / REVIEW:

DATE STARTED

DATE FINISHED

RATING

TITLE:

AUTHOR:

GENRE:

NOTES / REVIEW:

DATE STARTED

DATE FINISHED

RATING

TITLE:

AUTHOR:

GENRE:

NOTES / REVIEW:

Date started	Title:
	Author:
Date finished	Genre:
	Notes / Review:
Rating	
★★★★★	

Date started	Title:
	Author:
Date finished	Genre:
	Notes / Review:
Rating	
★★★★★	

Date started	Title:
	Author:
Date finished	Genre:
	Notes / Review:
Rating	
★★★★★	

DATE STARTED
_____

DATE FINISHED
_____

RATING
☆☆☆☆☆

TITLE:
AUTHOR:
GENRE:
NOTES / REVIEW:

DATE STARTED
_____

DATE FINISHED
_____

RATING
☆☆☆☆☆

TITLE:
AUTHOR:
GENRE:
NOTES / REVIEW:

DATE STARTED
_____

DATE FINISHED
_____

RATING
☆☆☆☆☆

TITLE:
AUTHOR:
GENRE:
NOTES / REVIEW:

Date started

_____

date finished

_____

rating
☆☆☆☆☆

TITLE:
AUTHOR:
GENRE:
NOTES / REVIEW:

Date started

_____

date finished

_____

rating
☆☆☆☆☆

TITLE:
AUTHOR:
GENRE:
NOTES / REVIEW:

Date started

_____

date finished

_____

rating
☆☆☆☆☆

TITLE:
AUTHOR:
GENRE:
NOTES / REVIEW:

DATE STARTED	TITLE:
DATE FINISHED	AUTHOR:
	GENRE:
	NOTES / REVIEW:
RATING ★★★★★	

DATE STARTED	TITLE:
DATE FINISHED	AUTHOR:
	GENRE:
	NOTES / REVIEW:
RATING ★★★★★	

DATE STARTED	TITLE:
DATE FINISHED	AUTHOR:
	GENRE:
	NOTES / REVIEW:
RATING ★★★★★	

Date started

_____

Date finished

_____

Rating

TITLE:

AUTHOR:

GENRE:

NOTES / REVIEW:

Date started

_____

Date finished

_____

Rating

TITLE:

AUTHOR:

GENRE:

NOTES / REVIEW:

Date started

_____

Date finished

_____

Rating

TITLE:

AUTHOR:

GENRE:

NOTES / REVIEW:

DATE STARTED	TITLE:
DATE FINISHED	AUTHOR:
	GENRE:
RATING	NOTES / REVIEW:

DATE STARTED	TITLE:
DATE FINISHED	AUTHOR:
	GENRE:
RATING	NOTES / REVIEW:

DATE STARTED	TITLE:
DATE FINISHED	AUTHOR:
	GENRE:
RATING	NOTES / REVIEW:

DATE STARTED

DATE FINISHED

RATING

TITLE:

AUTHOR:

GENRE:

NOTES / REVIEW:

DATE STARTED

DATE FINISHED

RATING

TITLE:

AUTHOR:

GENRE:

NOTES / REVIEW:

DATE STARTED

DATE FINISHED

RATING

TITLE:

AUTHOR:

GENRE:

NOTES / REVIEW:

Date started

Date finished

RATING

TITLE:
AUTHOR:
GENRE:
NOTES / REVIEW:

Date started

Date finished

RATING

TITLE:
AUTHOR:
GENRE:
NOTES / REVIEW:

Date started

Date finished

RATING

TITLE:
AUTHOR:
GENRE:
NOTES / REVIEW:

Date started

_____

date finished

_____

rating
★★★★★

TITLE:
AUTHOR:
GENRE:
NOTES / REVIEW:

Date started

_____

date finished

_____

rating
★★★★★

TITLE:
AUTHOR:
GENRE:
NOTES / REVIEW:

Date started

_____

date finished

_____

rating
★★★★★

TITLE:
AUTHOR:
GENRE:
NOTES / REVIEW:

DATE STARTED	TITLE:
DATE FINISHED	AUTHOR:
	GENRE:
RATING	NOTES / REVIEW:
★★★★★	

DATE STARTED	TITLE:
DATE FINISHED	AUTHOR:
	GENRE:
RATING	NOTES / REVIEW:
★★★★★	

DATE STARTED	TITLE:
DATE FINISHED	AUTHOR:
	GENRE:
RATING	NOTES / REVIEW:
★★★★★	

DATE STARTED

DATE FINISHED

RATING

TITLE:
AUTHOR:
GENRE:
NOTES / REVIEW:

DATE STARTED

DATE FINISHED

RATING

TITLE:
AUTHOR:
GENRE:
NOTES / REVIEW:

DATE STARTED

DATE FINISHED

RATING

TITLE:
AUTHOR:
GENRE:
NOTES / REVIEW:

Date started

date finished

rating

TITLE:
AUTHOR:
GENRE:
NOTES / REVIEW:

Date started

date finished

rating

TITLE:
AUTHOR:
GENRE:
NOTES / REVIEW:

Date started

date finished

rating

TITLE:
AUTHOR:
GENRE:
NOTES / REVIEW:

DATE STARTED	TITLE:
DATE FINISHED	AUTHOR:
	GENRE:
RATING	NOTES / REVIEW:

DATE STARTED	TITLE:
DATE FINISHED	AUTHOR:
	GENRE:
RATING	NOTES / REVIEW:

DATE STARTED	TITLE:
DATE FINISHED	AUTHOR:
	GENRE:
RATING	NOTES / REVIEW:

Date started

date finished

RATING

TITLE:
AUTHOR:
GENRE:
NOTES / REVIEW:

Date started

date finished

RATING

TITLE:
AUTHOR:
GENRE:
NOTES / REVIEW:

Date started

date finished

RATING

TITLE:
AUTHOR:
GENRE:
NOTES / REVIEW:

DATE STARTED

DATE FINISHED

RATING

TITLE:

AUTHOR:

GENRE:

NOTES / REVIEW:

DATE STARTED

DATE FINISHED

RATING

TITLE:

AUTHOR:

GENRE:

NOTES / REVIEW:

DATE STARTED

DATE FINISHED

RATING

TITLE:

AUTHOR:

GENRE:

NOTES / REVIEW:

DATE STARTED

DATE FINISHED

RATING

TITLE:
AUTHOR:
GENRE:
NOTES / REVIEW:

DATE STARTED

DATE FINISHED

RATING

TITLE:
AUTHOR:
GENRE:
NOTES / REVIEW:

DATE STARTED

DATE FINISHED

RATING

TITLE:
AUTHOR:
GENRE:
NOTES / REVIEW:

DATE STARTED

DATE FINISHED

RATING

TITLE:

AUTHOR:

GENRE:

NOTES / REVIEW:

DATE STARTED

DATE FINISHED

RATING

TITLE:

AUTHOR:

GENRE:

NOTES / REVIEW:

DATE STARTED

DATE FINISHED

RATING

TITLE:

AUTHOR:

GENRE:

NOTES / REVIEW:

Date started

Date finished

Rating

TITLE:
AUTHOR:
GENRE:
NOTES / REVIEW:

Date started

Date finished

Rating

TITLE:
AUTHOR:
GENRE:
NOTES / REVIEW:

Date started

Date finished

Rating

TITLE:
AUTHOR:
GENRE:
NOTES / REVIEW:

DATE STARTED

_____

DATE FINISHED

_____

RATING

☆☆☆☆☆

TITLE:
AUTHOR:
GENRE:
NOTES / REVIEW:

DATE STARTED

_____

DATE FINISHED

_____

RATING

☆☆☆☆☆

TITLE:
AUTHOR:
GENRE:
NOTES / REVIEW:

DATE STARTED

_____

DATE FINISHED

_____

RATING

☆☆☆☆☆

TITLE:
AUTHOR:
GENRE:
NOTES / REVIEW:

Date started

date finished

rating

TITLE:
AUTHOR:
GENRE:
NOTES / REVIEW:

Date started

date finished

rating

TITLE:
AUTHOR:
GENRE:
NOTES / REVIEW:

Date started

date finished

rating

TITLE:
AUTHOR:
GENRE:
NOTES / REVIEW:

DATE STARTED	TITLE:
	AUTHOR:
DATE FINISHED	GENRE:
	NOTES / REVIEW:
RATING ★★★★★	

DATE STARTED	TITLE:
	AUTHOR:
DATE FINISHED	GENRE:
	NOTES / REVIEW:
RATING ★★★★★	

DATE STARTED	TITLE:
	AUTHOR:
DATE FINISHED	GENRE:
	NOTES / REVIEW:
RATING ★★★★★	

DATE STARTED

DATE FINISHED

RATING

TITLE:
AUTHOR:
GENRE:
NOTES / REVIEW:

DATE STARTED

DATE FINISHED

RATING

TITLE:
AUTHOR:
GENRE:
NOTES / REVIEW:

DATE STARTED

DATE FINISHED

RATING

TITLE:
AUTHOR:
GENRE:
NOTES / REVIEW:

DATE STARTED

_____

DATE FINISHED

_____

RATING
★ ★ ★ ★ ★

TITLE:

AUTHOR:

GENRE:

NOTES / REVIEW:

DATE STARTED

_____

DATE FINISHED

_____

RATING
★ ★ ★ ★ ★

TITLE:

AUTHOR:

GENRE:

NOTES / REVIEW:

DATE STARTED

_____

DATE FINISHED

_____

RATING
★ ★ ★ ★ ★

TITLE:

AUTHOR:

GENRE:

NOTES / REVIEW:

DATE STARTED

DATE FINISHED

RATING

TITLE:

AUTHOR:

GENRE:

NOTES / REVIEW:

DATE STARTED

DATE FINISHED

RATING

TITLE:

AUTHOR:

GENRE:

NOTES / REVIEW:

DATE STARTED

DATE FINISHED

RATING

TITLE:

AUTHOR:

GENRE:

NOTES / REVIEW:

Date started

_____

Date finished

_____

rating
★ ★ ★ ★ ★

Title:
Author:
Genre:
Notes / Review:

Date started

_____

Date finished

_____

rating
★ ★ ★ ★ ★

Title:
Author:
Genre:
Notes / Review:

Date started

_____

Date finished

_____

rating
★ ★ ★ ★ ★

Title:
Author:
Genre:
Notes / Review:

DATE STARTED

DATE FINISHED

RATING

TITLE:
AUTHOR:
GENRE:
NOTES / REVIEW:

DATE STARTED

DATE FINISHED

RATING

TITLE:
AUTHOR:
GENRE:
NOTES / REVIEW:

DATE STARTED

DATE FINISHED

RATING

TITLE:
AUTHOR:
GENRE:
NOTES / REVIEW:

DATE STARTED

_____

DATE FINISHED

_____

RATING
★ ★ ★ ★ ★

TITLE:
AUTHOR:
GENRE:
NOTES / REVIEW:

DATE STARTED

_____

DATE FINISHED

_____

RATING
★ ★ ★ ★ ★

TITLE:
AUTHOR:
GENRE:
NOTES / REVIEW:

DATE STARTED

_____

DATE FINISHED

_____

RATING
★ ★ ★ ★ ★

TITLE:
AUTHOR:
GENRE:
NOTES / REVIEW:

Date started

_____

Date finished

_____

Rating

☆☆☆☆☆

TITLE:

AUTHOR:

GENRE:

NOTES / REVIEW:

Date started

_____

Date finished

_____

Rating

☆☆☆☆☆

TITLE:

AUTHOR:

GENRE:

NOTES / REVIEW:

Date started

_____

Date finished

_____

Rating

☆☆☆☆☆

TITLE:

AUTHOR:

GENRE:

NOTES / REVIEW:

Date started

_____

Date finished

_____

Rating
★ ★ ★ ★ ★

Title:
Author:
Genre:
Notes / Review:

Date started

_____

Date finished

_____

Rating
★ ★ ★ ★ ★

Title:
Author:
Genre:
Notes / Review:

Date started

_____

Date finished

_____

Rating
★ ★ ★ ★ ★

Title:
Author:
Genre:
Notes / Review:

DATE STARTED	TITLE:
	AUTHOR:
DATE FINISHED	GENRE:
	NOTES / REVIEW:
RATING ★★★★★	

DATE STARTED	TITLE:
	AUTHOR:
DATE FINISHED	GENRE:
	NOTES / REVIEW:
RATING ★★★★★	

DATE STARTED	TITLE:
	AUTHOR:
DATE FINISHED	GENRE:
	NOTES / REVIEW:
RATING ★★★★★	

Date started

---

date finished

---

rating

TITLE:
AUTHOR:
GENRE:
NOTES / REVIEW:

Date started

---

date finished

---

rating

TITLE:
AUTHOR:
GENRE:
NOTES / REVIEW:

Date started

---

date finished

---

rating

TITLE:
AUTHOR:
GENRE:
NOTES / REVIEW:

DATE STARTED

DATE FINISHED

RATING

TITLE:
AUTHOR:
GENRE:
NOTES / REVIEW:

DATE STARTED

DATE FINISHED

RATING

TITLE:
AUTHOR:
GENRE:
NOTES / REVIEW:

DATE STARTED

DATE FINISHED

RATING

TITLE:
AUTHOR:
GENRE:
NOTES / REVIEW:

Date started

_____

Date finished

_____

Rating
★ ★ ★ ★ ★

Title: _____
Author: _____
Genre: _____
Notes / Review: _____
_____
_____
_____

Date started

_____

Date finished

_____

Rating
★ ★ ★ ★ ★

Title: _____
Author: _____
Genre: _____
Notes / Review: _____
_____
_____
_____

Date started

_____

Date finished

_____

Rating
★ ★ ★ ★ ★

Title: _____
Author: _____
Genre: _____
Notes / Review: _____
_____
_____
_____

DATE STARTED

DATE FINISHED

RATING

TITLE:

AUTHOR:

GENRE:

NOTES / REVIEW:

DATE STARTED

DATE FINISHED

RATING

TITLE:

AUTHOR:

GENRE:

NOTES / REVIEW:

DATE STARTED

DATE FINISHED

RATING

TITLE:

AUTHOR:

GENRE:

NOTES / REVIEW:

DATE STARTED

DATE FINISHED

RATING

TITLE:
AUTHOR:
GENRE:
NOTES / REVIEW:

DATE STARTED

DATE FINISHED

RATING

TITLE:
AUTHOR:
GENRE:
NOTES / REVIEW:

DATE STARTED

DATE FINISHED

RATING

TITLE:
AUTHOR:
GENRE:
NOTES / REVIEW:

Date started

_____

Date finished

_____

Rating
★ ★ ★ ★ ★

Title:
Author:
Genre:
Notes / Review:

Date started

_____

Date finished

_____

Rating
★ ★ ★ ★ ★

Title:
Author:
Genre:
Notes / Review:

Date started

_____

Date finished

_____

Rating
★ ★ ★ ★ ★

Title:
Author:
Genre:
Notes / Review:

DATE STARTED	TITLE:
DATE FINISHED	AUTHOR:
	GENRE:
RATING	NOTES / REVIEW:
★★★★★	

DATE STARTED	TITLE:
DATE FINISHED	AUTHOR:
	GENRE:
RATING	NOTES / REVIEW:
★★★★★	

DATE STARTED	TITLE:
DATE FINISHED	AUTHOR:
	GENRE:
RATING	NOTES / REVIEW:
★★★★★	

Date started	TITLE:
	AUTHOR:
Date finished	GENRE:
	NOTES / REVIEW:
Rating	
★★★★★	

Date started	TITLE:
	AUTHOR:
Date finished	GENRE:
	NOTES / REVIEW:
Rating	
★★★★★	

Date started	TITLE:
	AUTHOR:
Date finished	GENRE:
	NOTES / REVIEW:
Rating	
★★★★★	

DATE STARTED	TITLE:
	AUTHOR:
DATE FINISHED	GENRE:
	NOTES / REVIEW:
RATING	

DATE STARTED	TITLE:
	AUTHOR:
DATE FINISHED	GENRE:
	NOTES / REVIEW:
RATING	

DATE STARTED	TITLE:
	AUTHOR:
DATE FINISHED	GENRE:
	NOTES / REVIEW:
RATING	

Date started

_____

date finished

_____

rating
☆ ☆ ☆ ☆ ☆

TITLE: _____
AUTHOR: _____
GENRE: _____
NOTES / REVIEW: _____
_____
_____

Date started

_____

date finished

_____

rating
☆ ☆ ☆ ☆ ☆

TITLE: _____
AUTHOR: _____
GENRE: _____
NOTES / REVIEW: _____
_____
_____

Date started

_____

date finished

_____

rating
☆ ☆ ☆ ☆ ☆

TITLE: _____
AUTHOR: _____
GENRE: _____
NOTES / REVIEW: _____
_____
_____

DATE STARTED	TITLE:
	AUTHOR:
DATE FINISHED	GENRE:
	NOTES / REVIEW:
RATING ☆☆☆☆☆	

DATE STARTED	TITLE:
	AUTHOR:
DATE FINISHED	GENRE:
	NOTES / REVIEW:
RATING ☆☆☆☆☆	

DATE STARTED	TITLE:
	AUTHOR:
DATE FINISHED	GENRE:
	NOTES / REVIEW:
RATING ☆☆☆☆☆	

DATE STARTED

DATE FINISHED

RATING

TITLE:
AUTHOR:
GENRE:
NOTES / REVIEW:

DATE STARTED

DATE FINISHED

RATING

TITLE:
AUTHOR:
GENRE:
NOTES / REVIEW:

DATE STARTED

DATE FINISHED

RATING

TITLE:
AUTHOR:
GENRE:
NOTES / REVIEW:

DATE STARTED

DATE FINISHED

RATING

TITLE:

AUTHOR:

GENRE:

NOTES / REVIEW:

DATE STARTED

DATE FINISHED

RATING

TITLE:

AUTHOR:

GENRE:

NOTES / REVIEW:

DATE STARTED

DATE FINISHED

RATING

TITLE:

AUTHOR:

GENRE:

NOTES / REVIEW:

Date started

_____

Date finished

_____

Rating
☆☆☆☆☆

TITLE: _____
AUTHOR: _____
GENRE: _____
NOTES / REVIEW: _____
_____
_____
_____

Date started

_____

Date finished

_____

Rating
☆☆☆☆☆

TITLE: _____
AUTHOR: _____
GENRE: _____
NOTES / REVIEW: _____
_____
_____
_____

Date started

_____

Date finished

_____

Rating
☆☆☆☆☆

TITLE: _____
AUTHOR: _____
GENRE: _____
NOTES / REVIEW: _____
_____
_____
_____

DATE STARTED
_____

DATE FINISHED
_____

RATING
★ ★ ★ ★ ★

TITLE:
AUTHOR:
GENRE:
NOTES / REVIEW:

DATE STARTED
_____

DATE FINISHED
_____

RATING
★ ★ ★ ★ ★

TITLE:
AUTHOR:
GENRE:
NOTES / REVIEW:

DATE STARTED
_____

DATE FINISHED
_____

RATING
★ ★ ★ ★ ★

TITLE:
AUTHOR:
GENRE:
NOTES / REVIEW:

DATE STARTED	TITLE:
	AUTHOR:
DATE FINISHED	GENRE:
	NOTES / REVIEW:
RATING	
★★★★★	

DATE STARTED	TITLE:
	AUTHOR:
DATE FINISHED	GENRE:
	NOTES / REVIEW:
RATING	
★★★★★	

DATE STARTED	TITLE:
	AUTHOR:
DATE FINISHED	GENRE:
	NOTES / REVIEW:
RATING	
★★★★★	

DATE STARTED

DATE FINISHED

RATING
★ ★ ★ ★ ★

TITLE:
AUTHOR:
GENRE:
NOTES / REVIEW:

DATE STARTED

DATE FINISHED

RATING
★ ★ ★ ★ ★

TITLE:
AUTHOR:
GENRE:
NOTES / REVIEW:

DATE STARTED

DATE FINISHED

RATING
★ ★ ★ ★ ★

TITLE:
AUTHOR:
GENRE:
NOTES / REVIEW:

DATE STARTED	TITLE:
DATE FINISHED	AUTHOR:
	GENRE:
RATING	NOTES / REVIEW:

DATE STARTED	TITLE:
DATE FINISHED	AUTHOR:
	GENRE:
RATING	NOTES / REVIEW:

DATE STARTED	TITLE:
DATE FINISHED	AUTHOR:
	GENRE:
RATING	NOTES / REVIEW:

DATE STARTED	TITLE:
DATE FINISHED	AUTHOR:
	GENRE:
RATING	NOTES / REVIEW:

DATE STARTED	TITLE:
DATE FINISHED	AUTHOR:
	GENRE:
RATING	NOTES / REVIEW:

DATE STARTED	TITLE:
DATE FINISHED	AUTHOR:
	GENRE:
RATING	NOTES / REVIEW:

DATE STARTED	TITLE:
	AUTHOR:
DATE FINISHED	GENRE:
	NOTES / REVIEW:
RATING	
★★★★★	

DATE STARTED	TITLE:
	AUTHOR:
DATE FINISHED	GENRE:
	NOTES / REVIEW:
RATING	
★★★★★	

DATE STARTED	TITLE:
	AUTHOR:
DATE FINISHED	GENRE:
	NOTES / REVIEW:
RATING	
★★★★★	

DATE STARTED

DATE FINISHED

RATING

TITLE:
AUTHOR:
GENRE:
NOTES / REVIEW:

DATE STARTED

DATE FINISHED

RATING

TITLE:
AUTHOR:
GENRE:
NOTES / REVIEW:

DATE STARTED

DATE FINISHED

RATING

TITLE:
AUTHOR:
GENRE:
NOTES / REVIEW:

DATE STARTED

DATE FINISHED

RATING

TITLE:
AUTHOR:
GENRE:
NOTES / REVIEW:

DATE STARTED

DATE FINISHED

RATING

TITLE:
AUTHOR:
GENRE:
NOTES / REVIEW:

DATE STARTED

DATE FINISHED

RATING

TITLE:
AUTHOR:
GENRE:
NOTES / REVIEW:

DATE STARTED

DATE FINISHED

RATING
☆☆☆☆☆

TITLE:
AUTHOR:
GENRE:
NOTES / REVIEW:

DATE STARTED

DATE FINISHED

RATING
☆☆☆☆☆

TITLE:
AUTHOR:
GENRE:
NOTES / REVIEW:

DATE STARTED

DATE FINISHED

RATING
☆☆☆☆☆

TITLE:
AUTHOR:
GENRE:
NOTES / REVIEW:

Date started

_____

date finished

_____

rating
★ ★ ★ ★ ★

TITLE: _____
AUTHOR: _____
GENRE: _____
NOTES / REVIEW: _____
_____
_____
_____

Date started

_____

date finished

_____

rating
★ ★ ★ ★ ★

TITLE: _____
AUTHOR: _____
GENRE: _____
NOTES / REVIEW: _____
_____
_____
_____

Date started

_____

date finished

_____

rating
★ ★ ★ ★ ★

TITLE: _____
AUTHOR: _____
GENRE: _____
NOTES / REVIEW: _____
_____
_____
_____

Date started

_____

date finished

_____

rating

★ ★ ★ ★ ★

TITLE:

AUTHOR:

GENRE:

NOTES / REVIEW:

Date started

_____

date finished

_____

rating

★ ★ ★ ★ ★

TITLE:

AUTHOR:

GENRE:

NOTES / REVIEW:

Date started

_____

date finished

_____

rating

★ ★ ★ ★ ★

TITLE:

AUTHOR:

GENRE:

NOTES / REVIEW:

Made in United States
Orlando, FL
27 November 2022